OLIVES

OLIVES
A BOOK OF RECIPES

HELEN SUDELL

LORENZ BOOKS

First published in 2014 by Lorenz Books
an imprint of Anness Publishing Limited
108 Great Russell Street, London, WC1B 3NA
www.annesspublishing.com
www.lorenzbooks.com; info@anness.com

If you like the images in this book and would like to investigate
using them for publishing, promotions or advertising, please visit
our website www.practicalpictures.com for more information

A CIP catalogue record for this book is available from
The British Library

Publisher Joanna Lorenz
Editorial Director Helen Sudell
Designer Nigel Partridge
Illustrations Anna Koska

Photographers: Martin Brigdale, William Lingwood, Gus Filgate,
John Whitaker, Nicki Dowey, Sam Stowell, Tim Auty, Steve Moss,
Karl Adamson
Recipes by: Ghillie Basan, Joanna Farrow, Pepita Aris, Sally
Mansfield, Maxine Clark, Rena Salaman, Valentina Harris, Matthew
Drennan, Miguel de Castro e Silva, Alex Barker, Carla Capalbo,
Shirley Gill, Jennie Shapter

Printed and bound in China

COOK'S NOTES

• Bracketed terms are intended for American readers.

• For all recipes, quantities are given in both metric and imperial
measures and, where appropriate, in standard cups and spoons.
Follow one set of measures, but not a mixture, because they are
not interchangeable.

• Standard spoon and cup measures are level. 1 tsp = 5ml,
1 tbsp = 15ml, 1 cup = 250ml/8fl oz.

• Australian standard tablespoons are 20ml. Australian readers
should use 3 tsp in place of 1 tbsp for measuring small quantities.

• American pints are 16fl oz/2 cups. American readers should use
20fl oz/2.5 cups in place of 1 pint when measuring liquids.

• Electric oven temperatures in this book are for conventional
ovens. When using a fan oven, the temperature will probably need
to be reduced by about 10–20°C/20–40°F. Since ovens vary, you
should check with your manufacturer's instruction book for
guidance.

• The nutritional analysis given for each recipe is calculated per
portion (i.e. serving or item), unless otherwise stated. If the recipe
gives a range, such as Serves 4–6, then the nutritional analysis will
be for the smaller portion size, i.e. 6 servings. The analysis does not
include optional ingredients, such as salt added to taste.

• Medium (US large) eggs are used unless otherwise stated.

PUBLISHER'S NOTE

CONTENTS

INTRODUCTION

Black olives were described by Lawrence Durrell as: "A taste older than meat, older than wine. A taste as old as cold water". The silver-grey olive tree has probably been cultivated around the Mediterranean for 8,000 years and the trees live long; in the heart of Majorca some trees may be 1,000 years old. The olive tree has always been of major importance to the Mediterranean way of life; the olive flourishes where nothing else will grow, and

Below: Olive trees live for many hundreds of years.

bread and olives were once the diet of the poor. Today, olives and olive oil combine perfectly with pasta, many types of vegetables, meat, fish and fruit to form the key note of the Mediterranean diet.

OLIVE VARIETIES

A choice of green or black olives is standard with apéritifs, but the real variety is amazing. Tiniest of all are the Spanish *Arbequines*, a medley of green or purplish-grey, with a hint of rosemary. The medium-size, oil-rich *Manzilla* is Spain's and California's main olive. Look out for huge green Spanish *Gordals del Rey* ("the king's fat ones"), often perversely labelled "Queen's", and brine-packed *Perlas* from Aragon, French irregular, green *Picholines*, large, black, brined *Tanche* and smaller reddish brown *Nyons* olives, Italian dull bronze-green *Calabreses* and the Sicilian-style small cracked olives in

Above: Kalamata olives from Greece are rich and pungent.

brine, stuffed with red pepper. Best of all, many think, are the extra large purple *Kalamata* olives from Greece, with the flavour of the red wine vinegar used to cure them. Black Greek olives in brine are the model for Californian *Alfonso* olives.

Of the 700 or so varieties, some are favoured for oil and others for table olives. The range of olive colours largely reflects the stage of picking: green olives are unripe, firm and less oily; purply brown ones are ripe and the black ones are overripe, with a much softer texture, and mainly used for oil. A wrinkled olive will probably be sun-dried.

A HEALTH-GIVING FRUIT

Olives have achieved iconic status in recent years because of the phenomenon of the "Mediterranean Diet". High levels of monounsaturated fat and low levels of saturated fat contained within olives, among other factors, have contributed to a low incident of heart disease in the region. Olives are also high in the fat-soluble vitamins A and E, as well as in copper and calcium.

Taking olive oil has been recommended for centuries to aid digestion, help lower cholesterol and reduce the effects of alcohol. Other therapeutic effects for olive oil include stimulating bile secretion, thereby reducing the risk of gallstones; the antioxidants in olive oil may help to reduce blood pressure, and spreading olive oil on wounds can speed up healing.

COOKING WITH OLIVES

The first person who, having tasted a wild olive, saw it as a crop, must have been someone of vision, for the olive on a tree is decidedly bitter. They are treated to remove the bitterness before preserving in brine, oil or vinegar, often flavoured with herbs, spices or aromatics.

Olives have an affinity with many ingredients. As well as

Above: Plates of olives handed round with aperitifs are a perfect start to a meal with friends.

featuring in starters and being sprinkled in all kinds of hot and cold salads, they provide a pungent counterpoint to delicate fish dishes: they also set off richer meats, such as lamb, duck and beef. Plus, their intense flavour provides a welcome punctuation in simpler dishes using pasta, grains and breads.

Olives have a highly versatile role in the kitchen, and the olive recipes contained within this book are sure to inspire you to make the most of them.

Left: Green olives are unripe and will need to be prepared before they are sold.

TYPES OF OLIVE

There are literally hundreds of varieties of olives, and, just as grapes are grown depending on whether they are intended for the table or for wine, so olives are grown either for eating or for pressing into oil. Different varieties are also grown according to climate, soil and other geographical conditions, so that the olives you find in most supermarkets are usually only classified by their country of origin.

GREEN OLIVES
Whether olives are green or black is not a matter of type but of timing – all olives are green at first, they are simply the unripe fruit of the tree. Green olives contain less oil, which explains why they have a sharper flavour and firmer flesh than the fully ripened black olive. Being unripe, green olives are inedible unless they are treated to remove their bitter and indigestible starches.

Commercially, this is done by immersing olives in a soda solution and then packing them in brine. However, local growers often prepare their own olives, washing them every day for about 10 days in fresh water and then storing them in earthenware jars of brine mixed with herbs, spices and other aromatic ingredients. They are then left for up to a year to develop their distinctive colour and smooth texture before being sold.

Below: Purple olives are ready to eat and taste delicious.

Pitted (stoned) olives are also stuffed with pieces of cooked pimiento, slivers of almond, anchovy or roasted garlic and are popularly exported.

BLACK OLIVES
These fully ripe olives, being full of oil, are more rounded in flavour and softer-fleshed than green olives. They are picked when fully ripe, then fermented and oxidized to give a glossy black finish.

BROWN OR PURPLE OLIVES
These are simply olives caught halfway between green and black. They have more of the characteristic mellow flavour of the black olive, yet will retain a subtle sharpness.

OLIVE PASTE
Wonderful spread on toasted bread, olive paste is easy to make and will keep for up to a month in an airtight container.

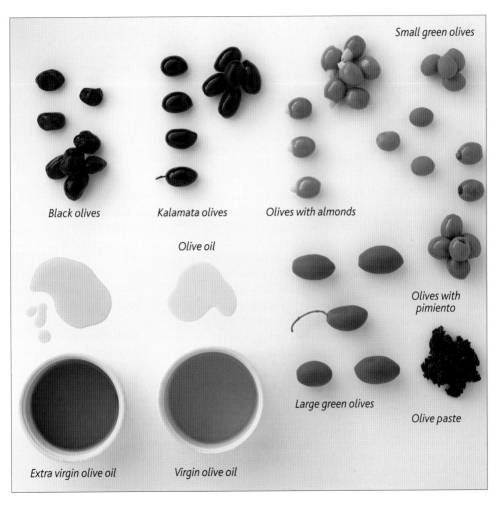

Small green olives

Black olives

Kalamata olives

Olives with almonds

Olive oil

Olives with pimiento

Large green olives

Olive paste

Extra virgin olive oil

Virgin olive oil

BASIC TECHNIQUES AND RECIPES

Preparing olives couldn't be simpler and requires a sharp knife or a special tool for getting rid of the olive stone.

PITTING OLIVES

1 Place the olive in the olive stoner, pointed end uppermost. Squeeze the two handles together to extract the stone.

2 Once pitted, the olives can be cut in half if they are to be used in salads or chopped finely.

MARINATING OLIVES

These are delicious to eat on their own, or add to casseroles or salads.

Crush 2.5ml/½ tsp coriander seeds with 2.5ml/½ tsp fennel seeds in a mortar and pestle. Work in 2 garlic cloves, then add 5ml/1 tsp chopped fresh rosemary, 10ml/2 tsp chopped fresh parsley, 15ml/1 tbsp sherry vinegar and 30ml/2 tbsp olive oil. Put 115g/4oz/⅔ cup each of black and green olives in a small bowl and pour over the marinade. Cover with cling film (plastic wrap) and chill for up to 1 week.

QUICK OLIVE IDEAS

For added flavour, add green olives to meat casseroles and stews.

Add assorted halved black olives to gremolata – a mixture of chopped parsley, lemon rind (zest) and crushed garlic. Mix with a little extra virgin olive oil and serve with hot pasta.

When making garlic bread, spread olive paste between the slices before baking.

Add chopped black olives to a vinaigrette dressing and serve with a green salad.

Use strips of olive to garnish savoury dishes.

Slice pimiento-stuffed olives horizontally and use to decorate fish dishes.

CRACKED GREEN OLIVES

Traditionally, cracked olives are slit or gently bruised before curing so that they absorb the curing ingredients faster.

Cut a cross at the top and bottom of 450g/1lb large green olives, cutting right through to the stone. Place a layer of olives in the bottom of one large, or several smaller sterilized jars, and sprinkle with 15ml/1 tbsp coriander seeds. Add a garlic clove, a slice of lemon, and 10ml/2 tsp oregano and continue making layers, leaving a good 2.5cm/1 in at the top of the jar. Fill with olive oil, cover tightly and leave to marinate for at least 2–3 weeks.

FETA CHEESE WITH OLIVES

A popular tapas favourite, feta cheese is delicious when marinated with spices and green pimiento olives. Placed in an attractive Kilner jar it also makes a wonderful gift.

Chop up 225g/8 oz/1 cup feta cheese into approximately 1.5cm/½ in cubes. Place in a bowl along with 20 green pimiento olives, sliced horizontally, 2 sprigs each of fresh thyme and rosemary plus 5ml/1 tsp coriander seeds. Mix together well and pour into sterilized jars. Fill with good quality extra virgin olive oil, cover tightly and leave to marinate for 2–3 weeks.

OLIVE TAPENADE

This black olive paste from Provence takes its name from the French word for capers.

Place 350g/12 oz pitted black olives, 1 can anchovies plus their oil, 30ml/2 tbsp capers, 1–2 crushed garlic cloves, 5ml/1 tsp chopped fresh thyme, 15ml/1 tbsp Dijon mustard, juice of ½ lemon and 45ml/3 tbsp olive oil in a food processor and blend until smooth. Turn into a dish and chill slightly before serving. Tapenade will keep for several days in a pot sealed with a layer of olive oil. Serve spread on crusted bread or as a dip for crisp vegetable sticks.

OLIVE OIL

Indisputably the king of oils, olive oil varies in flavour and colour, depending on how it is made and where it comes from. Of all the oils used in cooking, olive oil is considered to be the healthiest as it is rich in vitamins A and E, a natural antioxidant that can help fight off free radicals, which damage cells in the body. Olive oil is also a monounsaturated fat, which in many studies has been found to reduce 'bad' LDL cholesterol. All of these factors contribute to reducing the risk of heart disease and stroke.

Olive oils have as many flavours as there are varieties of olives. For the uninitiated, it is an almost impossible task to know what is a good oil, and each oil-producing country has its own system of labelling and grading. Colours vary from dark green to golden, yet are no indication of the quality of the oil, since it depends on where the olives were harvested. For those who are unsure about which olive oil to choose from the large selection available, the best method is to sample them in a hot dish, a salad, or dipped with chunks of bread, and then decide whether the flavour is one you prefer.

EXTRA VIRGIN OLIVE OIL
The best and most expensive olive oil is virgin oil from the first cold pressing. It has a very low acidity — less than 1 per cent. It is usually a greenish colour but may also be a light, golden yellow.

Extra virgin olive oil is not recommended for frying, as heat impairs its flavour, but it tastes wonderful in salad dressings, especially when combined with lighter oils. It is delicious as a sauce on its own, stirred into pasta with chopped garlic and black pepper, or simply drizzled over a plate of steamed vegetables.

Below: Cook with olive oil rather than butter as it is lower in saturated fat.

Below: Bread, olives, and virgin olive oil drizzled over cheese, is a typical Mediterranean meal.

Above: One of the simplest ways to enjoy truly great olive oil is to dunk pieces of bread into it.

VIRGIN OLIVE OIL

Also a pure first-pressed oil, this has a slightly higher level of acidity (up to 4 per cent) than extra virgin olive oil, and can be used in much the same way.

PURE OLIVE OIL

This is a blend of cold-pressed virgin oil and refined olive oil that has been treated with chemicals and then heated and filtered. The colour of the oil is normally paler and the flavour blander and less distinctive.

Light olive oil, which has a very mild flavour, is produced from the last pressing, and has the same nutritional values as pure olive oil. Because these oils are blended, each bottle will have the same mild flavour. These oils are suitable for all types of cooking and can be used for shallow frying. Where more flavour is required, for salad dressings or pasta sauces, virgin or extra virgin olive oil is the best option for an authentic Mediterranean taste. .

Below: Olive oil can also be infused with garlic, chillies or herbs to enhance its flavour.

QUICK MARINADES

Mix olive oil with chopped fresh herbs such as parsley, chives, oregano, chervil and basil. Add a splash or two of lemon juice and season with salt and pepper.

Combine groundnut (peanut) oil, toasted sesame oil, dark soy sauce, sweet sherry, rice vinegar and crushed garlic. Use as a marinade for tofu or tempeh.

Mix together olive oil, lemon juice, sherry honey and crushed garlic, and use as a marinade for vegetable and halloumi kebabs.

STARTERS
AND SALADS

OLIVES, WHETHER BLACK OR GREEN, WHOLE,

CHOPPED OR PURÉED, ADD THE TASTE OF THE

SUN-DRENCHED MEDITERRANEAN TO

COLOURFUL STARTERS AND FRESH SALADS

RED PEPPER AND OLIVE TAPENADE

Ciabatta toast with glorious paste of salty black olives, a little roasted garlic and the silken texture of sweet red peppers is a marriage made in heaven.

Serves 6

1 small red (bell) pepper
3 whole garlic cloves, skins on
225g/8oz black olives, pitted
30–45ml/2–3 tbsp salted capers or capers in vinegar, rinsed
12 drained canned anchovy fillets
about 150ml/¼ pint/⅔ cup good quality olive oil
fresh lemon juice and ground black pepper, to taste
45ml/3 tbsp chopped fresh basil
1 plain or black olive ciabatta, toasted, for serving

Energy 219kcal/903kJ; Protein 3.2g;
Carbohydrate 2.7g, of which sugars 1.8g;
Fat 21.8g, of which saturates 3.2g;
Cholesterol 5mg; Calcium 70mg;
Fibre 2.2g; Sodium 1173mg.

Place the whole pepper and garlic cloves under a hot grill (broiler) and grill (broil) for 15 minutes, turning, until charred all over. Once charred, put the garlic and pepper in a plastic bag, seal and leave to cool for about 10 minutes.

When the pepper is cool, lightly rub off the skin and remove the stalk and seeds. Peel the skin off the garlic. Place the pepper, garlic, olives and capers in a food processor with the anchovies and process until roughly chopped. With the machine running, slowly add the olive oil until you have a fairly smooth dark paste. Season to taste with lemon juice and pepper. Stir in the basil. Spread the paste on the finger toasts, or, if not using immediately, transfer to a sterilized jar, cover with a layer of olive oil and keep in the refrigerator for up to three weeks.

OLIVE AND ANCHOVY BITES

These little melt-in-the-mouth morsels are very easy to make, look impressive and are so moreish your dinner party guests will keep coming back for more.

Makes 40–45

115g/4oz/1 cup plain
  (all-purpose) flour
115g/4oz/½ cup chilled
  butter, diced
115g/4oz/1 cup finely grated
  Manchego, mature (sharp)
  Cheddar or Gruyère cheese
50g/2oz can anchovy fillets
  in oil, drained and roughly
  chopped
50g/2oz/½ cup pitted black
  olives, roughly chopped
2.5ml/½ tsp cayenne pepper
sea salt, to serve

Place the flour, butter, cheese, anchovies, olives and cayenne pepper in a food processor and pulse until the mixture forms a firm dough.

Wrap the dough loosely in clear film (plastic wrap). Chill for about 20 minutes.

Preheat the oven to 200°C/400°F/Gas 6. Roll out the dough thinly on a lightly floured surface.

Cut the dough into 5cm/2in wide strips, then cut across each strip in alternate directions, to make triangles. Transfer to baking sheets and bake for 8–10 minutes until golden. Cool on a wire rack. Sprinkle with sea salt.

Energy 42kcal/173kJ; Protein 1.2g; Carbohydrate 2g, of which sugars 0.1g; Fat 3.2g, of which saturates 1.9g; Cholesterol 9mg; Calcium 27mg; Fibre 0.1g; Sodium 103mg.

VARIATION
• To add a little extra spice, dust the olive and anchovy bites lightly with cayenne pepper before baking.
• Serve these bites alongside little bowls of lightly toasted sunflower seeds and pistachios.

STUFFED DEEP-FRIED GIANT OLIVES

These stuffed olives are usually served either as part of an antipasto or alongside a meat recipe as a delicious side dish. They are best served just warm, but are also good cold.

Serves 6

60 giant green olives
115g/4oz pork fat
60ml/4 tbsp extra virgin olive oil
150g/5oz/²⁄₃ cup minced (ground) pork
115g/4oz/¹⁄₂ cup minced (ground) beef
15ml/1 tbsp tomato purée (paste)
3 chicken livers
45ml/3 tbsp fresh white breadcrumbs
45ml/3 tbsp beef stock
1 egg, beaten
50g/2oz/²⁄₃ cup freshly grated Parmesan cheese
pinch freshly grated nutmeg
75ml/5 tbsp plain (all-purpose) flour
2 eggs beaten with 15ml/1 tbsp milk
65g/2¹⁄₂oz/1 cup dry breadcrumbs
vegetable oil, for deep-frying
salt and ground black pepper
lemon wedges, to serve

Stone (pit) all the olives carefully. It is important to keep them whole and as tidy as possible. Discard the stones (pits).

In a frying pan, heat the pork fat with the oil, then add the minced pork and beef, and cook for about 5 minutes until the meat is browned all over.

Add the tomato purée to the pan. Mix well, and cook for about 20 minutes, stirring occasionally.

Trim and chop the chicken livers, add to the pan and cook for a further 10 minutes.

Allow the liver and mince mixture to cool, and then chop the mixture finely using a heavy knife.

Add the breadcrumbs, stock, beaten egg and Parmesan cheese to the mixture. Add the nutmeg and season with salt and pepper.

Carefully, using your fingers, fill each olive with a little of the meat mixture.

Roll the olives in the flour, then in the beaten egg and milk, and then in the dry breadcrumbs.

Half fill a heavy pan with oil. If using a deep-fryer, fill it to the level recommended in the instruction book. Heat the oil to 180°C/350°F or until a cube of bread, added to the oil, turns golden in about 45 seconds.

Add the olives, in batches, to the hot oil and deep-fry until golden brown. Drain the olives on kitchen paper and serve hot or cold with the lemon wedges.

Energy 602kcal/2488kJ; Protein 18.2g; Carbohydrate 6.2g, of which sugars 0.5g; Fat 55.6g, of which saturates 15.8g; Cholesterol 210mg; Calcium 151mg; Fibre 1.2g; Sodium 983mg.

OLIVE AND PEPPER SALAD

Almost every hillside in the eastern Mediterranean is dotted with olive trees. Olives appear on most mezze tables, marinated in oil and herbs or spices, or tossed in a refreshing salad.

Serves 4–6

2 long, red Mediterranean
    peppers, or red or orange
    (bell) peppers
30–45ml/2–3 tbsp Kalamata or
    other fleshy black olives
30–45ml/2–3 tbsp fleshy green
    olives
1 large tomato, skinned, seeded
    and diced
2 spring onions (scallions),
    trimmed and finely sliced
small handful of fresh mint
    leaves, roughly chopped
small bunch of fresh coriander
    (cilantro), roughly chopped
30ml/2 tbsp olive oil
juice of 1 lemon
salt and ground black pepper
pitta bread, to serve

Place the peppers on a hot griddle, or directly over a gas flame or charcoal grill, turning until the skin is evenly charred. Leave them in a plastic bag for a few minutes to sweat, then hold each one under cold running water and peel off the skin. Remove the stalks and seeds, dice the flesh and place in a bowl.

Pit the olives and slice them in half lengthways. Add the halves to the bowl with the chopped peppers.

Add the tomato, spring onions and herbs and pour in the oil and lemon juice. Season and toss well. Serve with warm pitta bread as part of a mezze spread.

Energy 68kcal/283kJ; Protein 1.1g; Carbohydrate 4.6g, of which sugars 4.4g; Fat 5.2g, of which saturates 0.8g; Cholesterol 0mg; Calcium 30mg; Fibre 1.9g; Sodium 232mg

CABBAGE SALAD WITH BLACK OLIVES

This simple salad is made with a compact creamy-coloured "white" cabbage. It produces a rather sweet tasting, unusual salad, which has a crisp and refreshing texture.

Serves 4
1 white cabbage
12 black olives, pitted

For the dressing
75–90ml/5–6 tbsp extra virgin olive oil
30ml/2 tbsp lemon juice
1 garlic clove, crushed
30ml/2 tbsp finely chopped fresh flat leaf parsley
salt

Energy 307kcal/1269kJ; Protein 3.9g;
Carbohydrate 12.8g, of which sugars 12.5g;
Fat 26.9g, of which saturates 3.8g;
Cholesterol 0mg; Calcium 145mg; Fibre
5.8g; Sodium 21mg.

Cut the cabbage in quarters, discard the outer leaves and trim off any thick, hard stems as well as the hard base.

Lay each quarter in turn on its side and cut long, very thin slices until you reach the central core, which should be discarded. The key to a perfect cabbage salad is to shred the cabbage as finely as possible. Place the shredded cabbage in a bowl and stir in the black olives.

Make the dressing by whisking the olive oil, lemon juice, garlic, chopped parsley and salt to taste together in a bowl until well blended. Pour the dressing over the salad, and toss the cabbage and olives until everything is evenly coated.

ROCKET SALAD WITH BLACK OLIVES AND GARLIC

Serve this light but distinctively flavoured salad as a well-rounded first course or as an accompaniment to rare roast beef.

Serves 6

1 garlic clove, halved
115g/4oz good white bread, sliced
45ml/3 tbsp olive oil, plus extra for frying
75g/3oz rocket (arugula) leaves
75g/3oz baby spinach
25g/1oz flat leaf parsley, leaves only
45ml/3 tbsp salted capers, rinsed and dried
40g/1½ oz Parmesan cheese, shaved

For the dressing

25ml/5 tsp black olive paste
1 garlic clove, finely chopped
5ml/1 tsp Dijon mustard
75ml/5 tbsp olive oil
10ml/2 tsp balsamic vinegar
ground black pepper

Energy 262kcal/1084kJ; Protein 9.8g;
Carbohydrate 12.7g, of which sugars 3.5g;
Fat 19.3g, of which saturates 3.7g;
Cholesterol 7mg; Calcium 437mg; Fibre
4.5g; Sodium 565mg.

To make the dressing, whisk together the olive paste, garlic and mustard and gradually whisk in the oil, then the vinegar. Season to taste with black pepper.

Heat the oven to 190°C/375°F/Gas 5. Rub the garlic clove over the bread and cut the slices into croutons. Toss them in the oil and bake on a baking tray for 10–15 minutes until golden brown.

Mix the rocket, spinach and parsley in a salad bowl. Heat some olive oil in a pan and fry the capers briefly until crisp. Drain on kitchen paper. Toss the dressing and croutons into the salad and scatter the Parmesan and capers over the top. Serve immediately.

FISH, MEAT
AND POULTRY

TOGETHER WITH TOMATOES AND HERBS, OLIVES

ARE THE PERFECT PARTNER FOR FISH, AND ARE A

DELICIOUS ADDITION TO SIMPLE CHICKEN DISHES.

THEY ALSO COMBINE WELL WITH MORE COMPLEX

RICH MEATS SUCH AS DUCK OR BEEF

SALAD NIÇOISE

Made with the freshest of ingredients, this classic Provençal salad makes a simple yet unbeatable summer dish. Serve with country-style bread and chilled white wine.

Serves 4

*115g/4oz French beans,
    trimmed and cut in half*
115g/4oz mixed salad leaves
*½ small cucumber, thinly sliced
    crossways*
4 ripe tomatoes, quartered
*50g/2oz can anchovies, drained
    and halved lengthways*
4 eggs, hard-boiled
1 tuna steak, about 175g/6oz
olive oil, for brushing
*½ bunch small radishes,
    trimmed*
*50g/2oz/1½ cup small black
    olives*
salt and ground black pepper

For the dressing

90ml/6 tbsp extra virgin olive oil
2 garlic cloves, crushed
15ml/1 tbsp white wine vinegar

Energy 578kcal/2408kJ; Protein 46.4g;
Carbohydrate 15g, of which sugars 10.6g;
Fat 37.5g, of which saturates 7.1g;
Cholesterol 235mg; Calcium 127mg; Fibre
4.7g; Sodium 585mg.

To make the dressing, whisk together the oil, garlic and vinegar and season to taste with salt and pepper. Set aside.

Cook the French beans in a pan of boiling water for 2 minutes until just tender, then drain.

Mix together the salad leaves, sliced cucumber, tomatoes and French beans in a large, shallow bowl. Halve the anchovies lengthways and shell and quarter the eggs.

Preheat the grill (broiler). Brush the tuna steak with olive oil and sprinkle with salt and black pepper. Grill (broil) for 3–4 minutes on each side until cooked through. Allow to cool, then flake with a fork.

Scatter the flaked tuna, anchovies, quartered eggs, radishes and olives over the salad. Pour over the dressing and toss together lightly to combine. Serve at once.

BOURRIDE OF RED MULLET AND FENNEL WITH OLIVES

This fish soup, from Provence in France, is made with fresh mayonnaise. The secret of success is to cook the soup gently so the flavours combine.

Serves 4

25ml/1½ tbsp olive oil
1 onion, chopped
3 garlic cloves, chopped
2 fennel bulbs, halved, cored
    and thinly sliced
4 tomatoes, chopped
1 bay leaf
1 sprig fresh thyme
1.2 litres/2 pints/5 cups fish
    stock
675g/1½lb red mullet, scaled
    and filleted
8 slices baguette
1 garlic clove
30ml/2 tbsp sun-dried tomato
    paste
12 black olives, stoned and
    quartered
salt and ground black pepper
fresh fennel fronds, to garnish

For the mayonnaise

2 egg yolks
10ml/2 tsp white wine vinegar
300ml/½ pint/1¼ cups extra
    virgin olive oil

Heat the olive oil in a large, heavy-based saucepan. Add the chopped onion and garlic and cook for 5 minutes. Add the fennel and cook for a further 2–3 minutes. Stir in the tomatoes, bay leaf, thyme and fish stock. Bring the mixture to the boil, then reduce the heat and simmer for 30 minutes.

Meanwhile, make the mayonnaise. Put the egg yolks and vinegar in a bowl. Season and whisk well. Whisk in the oil, a little at a time. As the mayonnaise begins to emulsify and thicken, increase the speed with which you add the oil, from a few drops at a time to a slow trickle. Transfer to a large bowl and set aside.

Cut each mullet fillet into two or three pieces, then add them to the soup and cook gently for 5 minutes. Use a draining spoon to remove the mullet and set aside.

Strain the cooking liquid through a fine sieve. Whisk a ladleful of the soup into the mayonnaise, then whisk in the remaining soup in one go.

Return the soup to a clean pan and cook very gently, whisking continuously, until the mixture is very slightly thickened. Add the mullet to the soup and set it aside.

Toast the baguette slices on both sides. Rub each slice with the clove of garlic and spread with sun-dried tomato paste. Divide the olives among the toasted bread slices.

Very gently reheat the soup, but do not allow it to boil, then ladle it into bowls. Top each portion with two toasts and garnish with fennel.

Energy 322kcal/1354kJ; Protein 35.3g; Carbohydrate 17.5g, of which sugars 6.4g; Fat 12.9g, of which saturates 1g; Cholesterol 0mg; Calcium 173mg; Fibre 4.4g; Sodium 299mg.

TAGINE OF MONKFISH, CHERRY TOMATOES AND OLIVES

The fish for this tagine is marinated in chermoula, which gives it that unmistakable Moroccan flavour. It is a delightful dish at any time of year, served with lots of crusty bread.

Serves 4

900g/2lb monkfish tail, cut
* into chunks*
15–20 small new potatoes,
* scrubbed, scraped or peeled*
45–60ml/3–4 tbsp olive oil
4–5 garlic cloves, thinly sliced
15–20 cherry tomatoes
2 green (bell) peppers, grilled
* (broiled) until black, skinned,*
* seeded and cut into strips*
large handful of kalamata or
* fleshy black olives*
about 100ml/3½fl oz/scant ½
* cup water*
salt and ground black pepper
crusty bread, to serve

For the chermoula

2 garlic cloves
5ml/1 tsp coarse salt
10ml/2 tsp ground cumin
5ml/1 tsp paprika
juice of 1 lemon
small bunch of fresh coriander
* (cilantro), roughly chopped*
15ml/1 tbsp olive oil

Use a mortar and pestle to make the chermoula: pound the garlic with the salt to a smooth paste. Add the cumin, paprika, lemon juice and fresh coriander, and gradually mix in the olive oil to emulsify the mixture slightly. Reserve a little chermoula for cooking, then rub the rest of the paste over the chunks of monkfish. Cover and leave to marinate for about 1 hour.

Par-boil the potatoes for about 10 minutes until slightly softened. Drain, refresh under cold water and drain again, then cut them in half lengthways. Heat the olive oil in a heavy pan and stir in the garlic. When the garlic begins to colour, add the tomatoes and cook until just softened. Add the peppers and the remaining chermoula, and season with salt and pepper.

Spread the potatoes over the base of a tagine, shallow pan or deep, ridged frying pan. Spoon three-quarters of the tomato and pepper mixture over and place the marinated fish chunks on top, with their marinade. Spoon the rest of the tomato and pepper mixture on top of the fish and add the olives. Drizzle a little extra olive oil over the dish and pour in the water. Heat until simmering, cover the tagine or pan with a lid and steam over a medium heat for about 15 minutes, or until the fish is cooked through. Serve with fresh, warm crusty bread to mop up the delicious juices.

Energy 174kcal/735kJ; Protein 33.7g; Carbohydrate 6.1g, of which sugars 5.9g; Fat 1.8g, of which saturates 0.4g; Cholesterol 81mg; Calcium 32mg; Fibre 2.5g; Sodium 134mg.

RED MULLET WITH ONION, PEPPER AND OLIVES

The distinctive flavour of olive oil is used in marinades and dressings, to roast meat and soften vegetables. It is a perfect match for all the intense flavours of Mediterranean food.

Serves 6

7.5ml/1½ tsp mild paprika
45ml/3 tbsp flour
120ml/4fl oz/½ cup olive oil
6 red mullet or snapper, filleted
2 aubergines (eggplant), sliced
2 red or yellow (bell) peppers,
    seeded and sliced
1 large red onion, thinly sliced
2 garlic cloves, sliced
15ml/1 tbsp sherry vinegar
juice of 1 lemon
brown sugar, to taste
15ml/1 tbsp chopped fresh
    oregano
18–24 black olives
45ml/3 tbsp chopped fresh flat
    leaf parsley
salt and ground black pepper

Energy 335kcal/1406kJ; Protein 13.9g;
Carbohydrate 18.4g, of which sugars 11.5g;
Fat 15.5g, of which saturates 1.4g;
Cholesterol 0mg; Calcium 166mg; Fibre
4.6g; Sodium 347mg.

Mix 5ml/1 tsp of the paprika with the flour and season with salt and pepper. Heat half the oil in a large pan. Coat the fish in the flour and fry for 4–5 minutes until browned. Place in a non-metallic dish. Add another 30ml/2 tbsp of the oil to the pan and fry the aubergines until soft and browned. Add to the fish.

Add another 30ml/2 tbsp oil to the pan and soften the peppers and onion. Add the garlic and remaining paprika and cook for a further 2 minutes. Stir in the vinegar and lemon juice with 30ml/2 tbsp water and bring to a simmer. Season with sugar to taste and add the oregano and olives.

Spoon the marinade over the fish. When cool, cover and leave in the refrigerator for several hours. Before serving, bring the dish back to room temperature and stir in the parsley.

PROVENÇAL BEEF AND OLIVE DAUBE

A daube is a French method of braising meat with wine and herbs. This version from the Nice area in the south of France has the delicious addition of black olives and tomatoes.

Serves 6

1.5kg/3–3½lb topside beef
225g/8oz lardons
225g/8oz carrots, sliced
1 bay leaf
1 thyme sprig
2 parsley stalks
3 garlic cloves, thinly sliced
225g/8oz/2 cups pitted black olives
400g/14oz can tomatoes
crusty bread, flageolet beans or pasta, to serve

For the marinade

120ml/4fl oz/½ cup extra virgin olive oil
1 onion, sliced
4 shallots, sliced
1 carrot, sliced
150ml/¼ pint/⅔ cup red wine
6 peppercorns
2 garlic cloves, thinly sliced
1 bay leaf
1 thyme sprig
2 parsley stalks
salt

To make the marinade, heat the oil in a large shallow pan, add the onion, shallots, and carrot. Cook for 2 minutes, then lower the heat and add the red wine, peppercorns, garlic, bay leaf, thyme and parsley stalks. Season with salt, then cover and leave to simmer gently for 15–20 minutes. Set aside.

Place the beef in a large glass or earthenware dish and pour over the cooled marinade. Cover the dish and leave to marinate in a cool place or in the refrigerator for 12 hours, turning the meat once or twice.

Preheat the oven to 160°C/ 325°F/Gas 3. Lift the meat out of the marinade and fit snugly into an ovenproof casserole. Add the lardons and carrots, along with the herbs and garlic. Strain in all the marinade. Cover the casserole with greaseproof (waxed) paper, then the lid and cook in the oven for 2½ hours.

Remove the casserole from the oven and stir in the olives and tomatoes. Re-cover the casserole, return to the oven and cook for a further 30 minutes. Serve the meat cut into thick slices, accompanied by crusty bread, beans or pasta.

Energy 505kcal/2118kJ; Protein 64.7g; Carbohydrate 5g, of which sugars 4.6g; Fat 25.4g, of which saturates 7.3g; Cholesterol 149mg; Calcium 58mg; Fibre 3.3g; Sodium 1544mg.

SPANISH-STYLE LAMB STEW WITH GREEN OLIVES

In this hearty Mediterranean stew the lamb is marinated overnight and then slowly cooked to create a deeply satisfying rich flavour. Serve with plain boiled rice to soak up all the juices.

Serves 4

900g/2lb boneless leg of lamb
45ml/3 tbsp olive oil
15g/½oz/1 tbsp butter
2 red onions, thickly sliced
8 garlic cloves, crushed whole
2–3 red chillies, sliced
2 red (bell) peppers, sliced
5–10ml/1–2 tsp paprika
15–30ml/1–2 tbsp sugar
400g/14oz can tomatoes
15–30ml/1–2 tbsp tomato
*   purée (paste)*
2–3 bay leaves
225g/8oz small green olives
300ml/½ pint/1¼ cups water
salt and ground black pepper
fresh flat leaf parsley, to garnish
cooked rice, to serve

For the marinade

250ml/8fl oz/1 cup red wine
250ml/8fl oz/1 cup port
120ml/4fl oz/½ cup rice vinegar
1 onion, roughly sliced
2 garlic cloves, crushed whole
8 black peppercorns

First make the marinade by mixing all the ingredients together in a large bowl. Cut the lamb into bitesize pieces, add to the bowl and mix in the marinade. Cover the bowl with clear film (plastic wrap) and leave to marinate in the refrigerator for at least 6 hours or overnight.

Lift the lamb out of the marinade and put it in another large bowl. Strain the marinade through a slotted spoon and set aside.

Heat the oil and butter in a large flameproof casserole. Add the meat, in batches if necessary, and fry until browned on all sides. Using a slotted spoon, lift the browned meat out of the pan and put aside.

Add the onions, garlic, chillies and peppers to the remaining oil in the pan and fry for about 5 minutes until they begin to colour. Stir in the paprika and sugar and return the meat to the pan. Add the tomatoes, tomato purée, bay leaves and olives. Pour in the reserved marinade and the water and bring to the boil. Reduce the heat, cover the pan and simmer gently for about 2 hours, adding a little extra water if the cooking liquid reduces too much.

Season the stew with salt and pepper to taste. Sprinkle with chopped parsley to garnish and serve with rice.

Energy 654kcal/2722kJ; Protein 47.4g; Carbohydrate 19.2g, of which sugars 16.7g; Fat 43.6g, of which saturates 15.8g; Cholesterol 179mg; Calcium 93mg; Fibre 5.4g; Sodium 1498mg.

ROAST PORK STUFFED WITH FIGS, OLIVES AND ALMONDS

Pork is a popular meat in Spain, and this recipe using olives, figs and nuts in the stuffing is of Catalan influence, where the combination of meat and fruit is quite common.

Serves 4

60ml/4 tbsp olive oil
1 onion, finely chopped
2 garlic cloves, chopped
75g/3oz/1½ cups fresh
    breadcrumbs
4 ready-to-eat dried figs,
    chopped
8 pitted green olives, chopped
25g/1oz/¼ cup flaked almonds
15ml/1 tbsp lemon juice
15ml/1 tbsp chopped fresh
    parsley
1 egg yolk
900g/2lb boned loin of pork
salt and ground black pepper

Energy 635kcal/2671kJ; Protein 57.5g;
Carbohydrate 47.7g, of which sugars 31.8g;
Fat 25.2g, of which saturates 5g;
Cholesterol 190mg; Calcium 213mg;
Fibre 7.4g; Sodium 383mg.

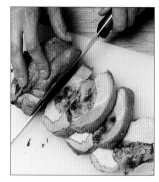

Preheat the oven to 200°C/400°F/Gas 6. Heat 45ml/3 tbsp of the oil in a pan, add the onion and garlic, and cook gently until softened. Remove the pan from the heat and stir in the breadcrumbs, figs, olives, almonds, lemon juice, parsley and egg yolk. Season to taste.

Remove any string from the pork and unroll the belly flap, cutting away any excess fat or meat, to enable you to do so. Spread half the stuffing over the flat piece and roll up, starting from the thick side. Tie at intervals with string.

Pour the remaining oil into a small roasting tin and put in the pork. Roast for 1 hour 15 minutes. Form the remaining stuffing mixture into balls and add to the roasting tin around the meat, 15–20 minutes before the end of cooking time.

Remove the pork from the oven and let it rest for 10 minutes. Carve into thick slices and serve with the stuffing balls and any juices from the tin. This is also good served cold.

CHICKEN TAGINE WITH GREEN OLIVES AND LEMON

This dish, which is particularly enjoyed in Marrakesh, celebrates two of Morocco's most famous ingredients – cracked green olives and preserved lemons.

Serves 4

1.3kg/3lb chicken
3 garlic cloves, crushed
small bunch of fresh coriander (cilantro), finely chopped
juice of ½ lemon
5ml/1 tsp coarse salt
45–60ml/3–4 tbsp olive oil
1 large onion, grated
pinch of saffron threads
5ml/1 tsp ground ginger
5ml/1 tsp ground black pepper
1 cinnamon stick
175g/6oz/1½ cups cracked green olives
2 preserved lemons, cut into strips
couscous, to serve

Energy 585kcal/2422kJ; Protein 40.4g;
Carbohydrate 0.4g, of which sugars 0.3g;
Fat 46.7g, of which saturates 11.7g;
Cholesterol 208mg; Calcium 68mg; Fibre
1.9g; Sodium 1151mg.

Place the chicken in a deep dish. Rub the garlic, fresh coriander, lemon juice and salt into the chicken cavity. Mix the olive oil with the grated onion, saffron, ginger and pepper and rub this mixture over the outside of the chicken. Cover and leave to stand for about 30 minutes.

Transfer the chicken to a tagine or large, heavy flameproof casserole and pour the marinating juices over. Pour in enough water to come halfway up the chicken, add the cinnamon stick and bring the water to the boil. Reduce the heat, cover with a lid and simmer for about 1 hour, turning the chicken occasionally.

Preheat the oven to 150°C/300°F/Gas 2. Using two slotted spoons, carefully lift the chicken out of the tagine or casserole and set aside on a plate, covered with foil. Turn up the heat and boil the cooking liquid for 5 minutes to reduce it. Replace the chicken in the liquid and baste it thoroughly. Add the olives and preserved lemon and place the tagine or casserole in the oven for about 15 minutes. Serve the chicken immediately with couscous.

DUCK WITH BLACK OLIVES

This dish successfully combines olives and mushrooms with duck. The white port imparts a subtle and authentic flavour to this traditional Portuguese dish.

Serves 4

*2 ducks, weighing about
    1.8 kg/4lb each
100ml/4fl oz/½ cup olive oil
5ml/1 tsp fresh rosemary leaves
50ml/2fl oz/¼ cup white port
200g/7oz oyster mushrooms,
    sliced
100g/3¾oz/ generous ½ cup
    diced cured ham
100g/3¾oz/generous ½ cup
    diced bacon
2 garlic cloves, chopped
200g/7oz/1¾ cups black olives
salt and ground black pepper
cabbage and potatoes, to serve*

Bone the ducks, separating the legs and the breasts with the wings. Put the bones in a large pan with 50ml/2fl oz/½ cup of the olive oil and cook, turning frequently, for about 10 minutes, until coloured.

Season the duck meat with salt and pepper and sprinkle with the rosemary. Add to the pan and cook until lightly coloured. Pour in the port and enough water just to cover. Bring just to the boil, then lower the heat, cover and simmer for 30 minutes.

Remove the meat with a slotted spoon and reserve. Remove and discard the bones. Skim off the fat from the surface of the cooking liquid and reserve the liquid.

Preheat the oven to 200°C/400°F/Gas 6. Heat the remaining olive oil in a pan. Add the mushrooms, ham and bacon and cook over a low heat, stirring occasionally, for 5 minutes. Add the garlic, olives and the reserved cooking liquid.

Put the vegetable mixture in a terracotta or other ovenproof dish. Add the duck legs and breasts, skin side up, on top and place them, uncovered, in the oven for 15 minutes to dry a little and gain some colour. Serve immediately, with cabbage and potatoes.

Energy 643kcal/2686kJ; Protein 69.2g; Carbohydrate 2g, of which sugars 1.9g; Fat 38.5g, of which saturates 9.9g; Cholesterol 358mg; Calcium 73mg; Fibre 2g; Sodium 2143mg.

VARIATION
If you can't find white port use brandy instead.

VEGETARIAN DISHES

OLIVES COMBINE BEAUTIFULLY WITH VEGETABLES,

WHETHER ROASTED IN OLIVE OIL OR AS PART OF

A SPICY PASTA SAUCE. CHEESE AND EGGS ARE

ALSO ENHANCED WITH THE RICHNESS OF

OLIVES IN TAGINES AND OMELETTES

NOODLES WITH GREEN OLIVES AND PARSLEY

This is a traditional Jewish dish. The egg noodles are dressed with garlic, parsley and olives and eaten as either a first course or as an accompaniment to fish.

Serves 4

250g/9 oz dried egg noodles
30–60ml/2–4 tbsp extra virgin olive oil
3 garlic cloves, finely chopped
60–90ml/4–6 tbsp roughly chopped fresh parsley
25–30 pitted green olives, sliced or roughly chopped
salt

Cook the noodles in salted boiling water as directed on the packet, or until just tender. Drain and rinse under cold running water.

Tip the pasta into a bowl, then add the olive oil, garlic, parsley and olives and toss together.

Chill overnight before serving.

Energy 352kcal/1476kJ; Protein 8.6g; Carbohydrate 45.3g, of which sugars 1.6g; Fat 16.4g, of which saturates 3.1g; Cholesterol 19mg; Calcium 86mg; Fibre 4.2g; Sodium 1244mg.

COOK'S TIP
Because this dish is so simple, always use the best quality ingredients.

PENNE, OLIVES AND SUN-DRIED TOMATOES

This delicious salad combines all the flavours of the Mediterranean. It is an excellent way of serving pasta and is particularly nice on hot summer days.

Serves 6

450 g/1 lb short pasta, such as medium shells, farfalle or penne
60 ml/4 tbsp extra-virgin olive oil
10 sun-dried tomatoes, thinly sliced
30 ml/2 tbsp capers, in brine or salted
115 g/4 oz/²⁄₃ cup black olives, pitted
2 cloves garlic, finely chopped
45 ml/3 tbsp balsamic vinegar
salt and ground black pepper
45 ml/3 tbsp chopped fresh parsley

Cook the pasta in a large pan of rapidly boiling salted water until it is *al dente*. Drain, and rinse under cold water to stop the cooking. Drain well and turn into a large bowl. Toss with the olive oil, and set aside.

Soak the tomatoes in a bowl of hot water for 10 minutes. Do not discard the water. Rinse the capers well. If they have been preserved in salt, soak them in a little hot water for 10 minutes. Rinse again.

Combine the olives, tomatoes, capers, garlic and vinegar in a small bowl. Season with salt and pepper.

Stir this mixture into the pasta, and toss well. Add 2 or 3 spoons of the tomato soaking water if the salad seems too dry. Toss with the parsley, and allow to stand for 15 minutes before serving.

Energy 353kcal/1491kJ; Protein 1.2g; Carbohydrate 57.3g, of which sugars 2.3g; Fat 14.2g, of which saturates 2.9g; Cholesterol 17mg; Calcium 27mg; Fibre 3.6g; Sodium 1013mg.

MOJETE

The Spanish love to scoop up cooked vegetables with bread, and here peppers, tomatoes and onions are baked together to make a colourful, soft vegetable dish that is studded with olives.

Serves 8

2 red (bell) peppers
2 yellow (bell) peppers
1 red onion, sliced
2 garlic cloves, halved
50g/2oz/¼ cup black olives
6 large ripe tomatoes, quartered
5ml/1 tsp soft light brown sugar
45ml/3 tbsp amontillado sherry
3–4 fresh rosemary sprigs
30ml/2 tbsp olive oil
salt and ground black pepper
crusty bread, to serve

Halve the peppers and remove the seeds. Cut each pepper lengthways into 12 strips. Preheat the oven to 200°C/400°F/Gas 6.

Place the peppers, onion, garlic, olives and tomatoes in a large roasting pan (tin).

Sprinkle the vegetables with the sugar, then pour in the sherry. Season well with salt and pepper, cover with foil and bake for 45 minutes.

Remove the foil from the pan and stir the mixture well. Add the rosemary sprigs and drizzle with the olive oil. Return the pan to the oven and cook for a further 30 minutes, uncovered, until the vegetables are very tender. Serve hot or cold with plenty of chunks of fresh crusty bread to soak up the liquid.

COOK'S TIP
Spain is the world's chief olive producer, with half the crop being exported. Try to use good quality Spanish olives for this recipe. Choose unpitted ones as they have a better flavour.

Energy 75kcal/313kJ; Protein 1.3g; Carbohydrate 7.5g, of which sugars 7.2g; Fat 3.9g, of which saturates 0.6g; Cholesterol 0mg; Calcium 17mg; Fibre 2g; Sodium 151mg.

TAGINE OF BUTTER BEANS, TOMATOES AND OLIVES

Serve this hearty butter bean dish with grills or roasts, particularly fish. It is also substantial enough to be served on its own, with a leafy salad and fresh, crusty bread.

Serves 4

*115g/4oz/²⁄₃ cup butter (lima)
  beans, soaked overnight
30–45ml/2–3 tbsp olive oil
1 onion, chopped
2–3 garlic cloves, crushed
25g/1oz fresh root ginger,
  peeled and chopped
pinch of saffron threads
16 cherry tomatoes
generous pinch of sugar
handful of fleshy black olives,
  pitted
5ml/1 tsp ground cinnamon
5ml/1 tsp paprika
small bunch of flat leaf parsley
salt and ground black pepper*

Energy 138kcal/578kJ; Protein 5.5g;
Carbohydrate 12.8g, of which sugars 3.5g;
Fat 7.6g, of which saturates 1.1g;
Cholesterol 0mg; Calcium 51mg; Fibre
5.2g; Sodium 605mg.

Rinse the beans and place them in a large pan with plenty of water. Bring to the boil and boil for about 10 minutes, then reduce the heat and simmer gently for 1–1½ hours until tender. Drain the beans and refresh under cold water.

Heat the olive oil in a heavy pan. Add the onion, garlic and ginger, and cook for about 10 minutes, or until softened but not browned. Stir in the saffron threads, followed by the cherry tomatoes and a sprinkling of sugar.

As the tomatoes begin to soften, stir in the butter beans. When the tomatoes have heated through, stir in the olives, ground cinnamon and paprika. Season to taste, chop the parsley and sprinkle over. Serve immediately.

Using canned beans: If you are in a hurry, you could use two 400g/14oz cans of butter beans for this tagine. Make sure you rinse the beans well before adding as canned beans tend to be salty.

SCALLOPED POTATOES WITH FETA CHEESE AND OLIVES

Thinly sliced potatoes are cooked with Greek feta cheese and black and green olives in olive oil. This dish is a good one to serve with toasted pitta bread.

Serves 4

900g/2lb main crop potatoes
150ml/¼ pint/⅔ cup olive oil
1 sprig rosemary
275g/10oz/2½ cups feta
cheese, crumbled
115g/4oz/1 cup pitted black
and green olives
300ml/½ pint/1¼ cups hot
vegetable stock
salt and ground black pepper

Preheat the oven to 200°C/400°F/Gas 6. Cook the potatoes in plenty of boiling water for 15 minutes. Drain and cool slightly. Peel the potatoes and cut into thin slices.

Brush the base and sides of a 1.5 litre/2½ pint/6¼ cup rectangular ovenproof dish with some of the olive oil.

Layer the potatoes in the dish with the rosemary, crumbled cheese and olives. Drizzle with the remaining olive oil and pour over the stock. Season the whole with salt and plenty of ground black pepper.

Cook for 35 minutes, covering with foil to prevent the potatoes from getting too brown. Serve hot, straight from the dish.

Energy 584kcal/2429kJ; Protein 14.8g; Carbohydrate 37.3g, of which sugars 4g; Fat 42.7g, of which saturates 13.7g; Cholesterol 48mg; Calcium 279mg; Fibre 3.1g; Sodium 1662mg.

COOK'S TIP
Make sure you choose Greek feta cheese, which has a completely different texture to Danish.

CHEESE OMELETTE WITH PEPPER AND OLIVES

This kind of thick omelette is often served as a snack, or cut into small portions as a mezze dish. On street stalls, omelettes are often cooked in large, wide pans and divided up for customers.

Serves 4–6

30ml/2 tbsp olive oil
1 red onion, chopped
1 green or red (bell) pepper,
    chopped
1 red chilli, seeded and chopped
225g/8oz feta cheese, crumbled
12 black olives, pitted and
    halved
small bunch of flat leaf parsley,
    chopped
small bunch of mint leaves,
    chopped
6 eggs, lightly beaten with
    about 50ml/2fl oz/¼ cup
    milk
ground black pepper

Heat the oil in a heavy non-stick pan and cook the onion, pepper and chilli until they begin to brown. Stir in the feta cheese, olives and herbs and quickly add in the beaten eggs. Season with pepper.

Pull the egg mixture into the middle of the pan to help it spread and cook evenly. Reduce the heat, cover the pan with a lid, or a piece of foil, and let the omelette cook gently for 5–10 minutes until it becomes thick and solid.

Drizzle a little extra oil over the top and brown it under a preheated grill (broiler), or in a hot oven, if you like. Cut the omelette into portions and serve hot or at room temperature.

Energy 303kcal/1252kJ; Protein 13.8g; Carbohydrate 5.5g, of which sugars 4.6g; Fat 25.4g, of which saturates 8.6g; Cholesterol 217mg; Calcium 230mg; Fibre 3.1g; Sodium 2304mg

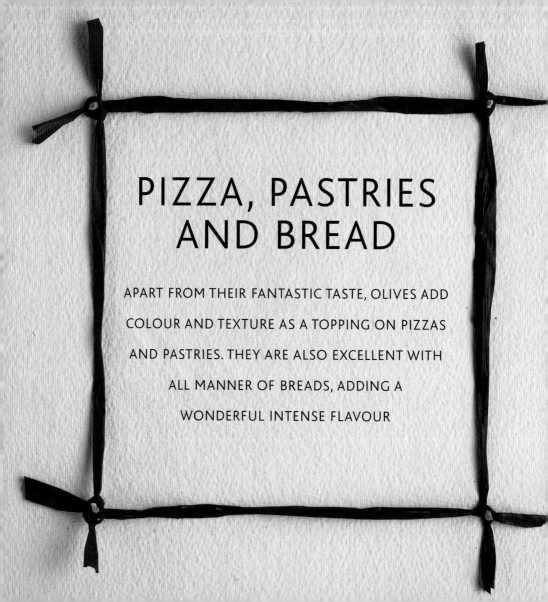

PIZZA, PASTRIES AND BREAD

APART FROM THEIR FANTASTIC TASTE, OLIVES ADD

COLOUR AND TEXTURE AS A TOPPING ON PIZZAS

AND PASTRIES. THEY ARE ALSO EXCELLENT WITH

ALL MANNER OF BREADS, ADDING A

WONDERFUL INTENSE FLAVOUR

FARMHOUSE PIZZA

This is the ultimate party pizza. Served cut into fingers, it is ideal for a crowd. For additional colour decorate the pizza with a mixture of black and green olives.

Serves 8

90 ml/6 tbsp olive oil

225 g/8 oz button mushrooms, sliced

2 quantities ready-made pizza dough

350 g/12 oz canned, chopped tomatoes

300 g/10 oz mozzarella, thinly sliced

115 g/4 oz wafer-thin smoked ham slices

6 bottled artichoke hearts in oil, drained and sliced

50 g/2 oz can anchovy fillets, drained and halved lengthways

10 pitted black olives, halved

30 ml/2 tbsp chopped fresh oregano

45 ml/3 tbsp freshly grated Parmesan

black pepper

Energy 377kcal/1574kJ; Protein 17.5g;
Carbohydrate 28.3g, of which sugars 3g;
Fat 22.4g, of which saturates 7.7g;
Cholesterol 38mg; Calcium 285mg;
Fibre 1g; Sodium 818mg.

Preheat the oven to 220°C/425°F/ Gas 7. Heat 30 ml/2 tbsp of the oil in a large frying pan, add the mushrooms and fry for about 5 minutes until all the juices have evaporated. Leave to cool.

Roll out the dough on a lightly floured surface to a 30 x 25cm/12 x 10 in rectangle. Transfer to a greased baking sheet then push up the dough edges to make a thin rim. Brush with 30 ml/2 tbsp of the oil.

Spread over the chopped tomatoes and arrange the sliced mozzarella over the sauce. Scrunch up the ham and arrange on top with the artichoke hearts, mushrooms and anchovies.

Dot with the olives, then sprinkle over the oregano and Parmesan. Drizzle over the remaining oil and season with black pepper. Bake for about 25 minutes until crisp and golden. Serve immediately.

RED ONION AND OLIVE PISSALADIÈRE

For a taste of the Mediterranean, try this French-style pizza – it makes a delicious snack. Cook the sliced red onions slowly until they are caramelized before piling them into the pastry cases.

Serves 6

75ml/5 tbsp extra virgin olive oil
500g/1¼ lb small red onions, thinly sliced
500g/1¼ lb puff pastry, thawed if frozen
75g/3oz/¾ cup small pitted black olives

Preheat the oven to 220°C/425°F/Gas 7. Heat the oil in a large, heavy frying pan and cook the onions gently, stirring frequently, for 15–20 minutes, until they are soft and golden. Season to taste.

Roll out the pastry thinly on a floured surface. Cut out a 33cm/13in round and transfer it to a lightly dampened baking sheet.

Spread the onions over the pastry in an even layer to within 1cm/½ in of the edge. Sprinkle the olives on top. Bake the tart for 20–25 minutes, until the pastry is risen and deep golden. Cut into wedges and serve while still warm.

Energy 436kcal/1815kJ; Protein 5.9g; Carbohydrate 37.4g, of which sugars 5.8g; Fat 31.1g, of which saturates 1.5g; Cholesterol 0mg; Calcium 77mg; Fibre 1.5g; Sodium 542mg.

COOK'S TIP
To prepare the recipe in advance, pile the cooled onions on to the pastry round and chill the pissaladière until you are ready to bake it.

TOMATO AND BLACK OLIVE TART

This colourful tart has a fresh, rich Mediterranean flavour and is perfect for picnics, but it can, of course, be made all year round, served with a crisp green salad.

Serves 8

375g/13oz shortcrust pastry, at room temperature
3 eggs, beaten
300ml/½ pint/1¼ cups milk
30ml/2 tbsp chopped fresh herbs, such as parsley, marjoram or basil
6 firm plum tomatoes
75g/3oz ripe Brie cheese
about 16 black olives, stoned
salt and ground black pepper

VARIATIONS
This tart is delicious made with other cheeses. Try slices of Gorgonzola or Camembert for a slightly stronger flavour or, alternatively, scatter a few strips of anchovy fillet over the tart before baking.

Preheat the oven to 190°C/375°F/Gas 5. Roll out the pastry thinly on a lightly floured surface. Line a 28 x 18cm/11 x 7in loose-based rectangular flan tin, trimming off any overhanging edges.

Line the pastry case with baking parchment and baking beans, and bake blind for 15 minutes. Remove the baking parchment and beans and bake for a further 5 minutes until the base is crisp.

Meanwhile, mix together the eggs, milk, seasoning and herbs. Slice the tomatoes, cube the cheese, and slice the olives. Place the prepared flan case on a baking tray, arrange the tomatoes, cheese and olives in the bottom of the case, then pour in the egg mixture. Transfer carefully to the oven and bake for about 40 minutes until just firm and turning golden. Slice hot or cool in the tin, then serve.

Energy 315kcal/1316kJ; Protein 9.3g; Carbohydrate 26.1g, of which sugars 4.6g; Fat 19.9g, of which saturates 7.2g; Cholesterol 90mg; Calcium 151mg; Fibre 1.7g; Sodium 505mg.

OLIVE AND ANCHOVY BREAD

This is a light loaf from Italy, perfect for tearing and sharing. Serve the bread as part of an antipasto course, with a richly dressed tomato salad and some salami and sliced prosciutto.

Serves 4–6

400g/14oz/3½ cups strong white bread flour
15g/½oz fresh (compressed) yeast
175ml/6fl oz/¾ cup olive oil
20 marinated green olives, pitted
7 or 8 salted anchovies, rinsed, boned and chopped
ground black pepper

Pile the flour on a clean work surface and plunge your fist in the top to make a hollow all the way through.

Mash the yeast in a small bowl with just enough water to make a thick liquid. Pour this into the hollow, add about one-third of the olive oil and knead together very thoroughly with your hands, making a dough that is as pliable and elastic as possible.

When the dough comes away easily from your hands, divide it into smallish lumps and roll each lump out to a disc that is about the size of a side plate. Place each dough disc on a separate plate, cover with cloths and leave in a warm place to rise until doubled in bulk. This should take about 30 minutes.

Preheat the oven to 180°C/350°F/Gas 4. Brush an oval baking dish, about 18cm/7 in in length, with some of the remaining oil. Knock back (punch down) the discs and flatten them. Scatter each disc with a few olives, a few pieces of anchovy and a little olive oil.

Roll a disc up loosely to make a tube shape about 2.5–3cm/1–1¼in thick, then stand it on end and push it down from the top to squash it slightly. Repeat for the remaining discs.

Stand all the squashed tubes side by side in the baking dish. Push them up tight against one another to make one big loaf. Brush the surface with oil and bake for 40 minutes, until the loaf is well risen and is golden brown. Remove from the dish and cool on a wire rack.

Energy 482kcal/2013kJ; Protein 7.8g; Carbohydrate 51.8g, of which sugars 1g; Fat 28.4g, of which saturates 3.9g; Cholesterol 0mg; Calcium 117mg; Fibre 2.4g; Sodium 456mg.

VARIATION
This bread can also accompany a selection of seafood dressed with olive oil, chilli and garlic.

OLIVE BREAD

Black and green olives and good-quality fruity olive oil combine to make this strongly flavoured and irresistible Italian bread. Serve with cold meats or to accompany soup.

Makes 1 loaf

275g/10oz/2½ cups strong white bread flour
50g/2oz/½ cup wholemeal (whole-wheat) bread flour
7g/¼ oz sachet easy bake (rapid-rise) dried yeast
2.5ml/½ tsp salt
210ml/7½ fl oz/ 1 cup lukewarm water
15ml/1 tbsp extra virgin olive oil, plus extra, for brushing
115g/4oz/1 cup pitted black and green olives, coarsely chopped

VARIATIONS
Increase the proportion of wholemeal flour to make the loaf more rustic.

Energy 1325kcal/5600kJ; Protein 31.6g;
Carbohydrate 252.5g, of which sugars 4.9g;
Fat 27.8g, of which saturates 4.2g;
Cholesterol 0mg; Calcium 525mg; Fibre
13.4g; Sodium 3557mg.

Lightly grease a baking sheet. Mix the flours, yeast and salt together in a large bowl and make a well in the centre. Add the water and oil to the centre of the flour and mix to a soft dough. Knead the dough on a lightly floured surface for 8–10 minutes until smooth and elastic. Place in a lightly oiled bowl, cover with lightly oiled clear film (plastic wrap) and leave in a warm place, for 1 hour, or until doubled in bulk.

Turn out on to a lightly floured surface and knock back (punch down). Flatten out and sprinkle over the olives. Fold up and knead to distribute the olives. Leave to rest for 5 minutes, then shape into an oval loaf. Place on the baking sheet.

Make six deep cuts in the top of the loaf, and gently push the sections over. Cover with lightly oiled clear film and leave to rise, in a warm place, for 30–45 minutes, or until doubled in size.

Meanwhile, preheat the oven to 200°C/400°F/Gas 6. Brush the bread with olive oil and bake for 35 minutes. Transfer to a wire rack to cool.

INDEX